No A9

Birds Fly, Bears Don't

THEODORE CLYMER
ROSELMINA INDRISANO
DALE D. JOHNSON
P. DAVID PEARSON
RICHARD L. VENEZKY

Consultants
CLAIRE HENRY
HUGHES MOIR
PHYLLIS WEAVER

Ginn and Company

0-663-38458-3

Acknowledgments: Grateful acknowledgment
is made to the following publishers, authors, and
agents for permission to use and adapt copy-
righted material:

David C. Cook Publishing Co. for the poem
"Grandpa" by Carolyn Joyce. © 1977 David C.
Cook Publishing Co., Elgin, IL 60120. Used by
permission.

Crown Publishers, Inc., for "Three Kittens"
by Mirra Ginsburg. Text adapted from *Three Kittens* by Mirra Ginsburg & Giuolo Maestro. Text
copyright © 1973 by Mirra Ginsburg. Used by
permission of Crown Publishers, Inc.

The Dial Press for "Head In, Head Out" by
Frank Asch. Adapted from *Turtle Tale* by Frank
Asch. Copyright © 1978 by Frank Asch.
Reprinted by permission of The Dial Press.

Ginn and Company for the song "Baby
Chicks" by Norma VanZee. From *The Magic of
Music — Book One,* © Copyright, 1970, 1965,
by Ginn and Company (Xerox Corporation).
Used with permission.

Hamish Hamilton Limited, London, for "The
Chick and the Duckling" adapted from *The
Chick and the Duckling* by Mirra Ginsburg.
Copyright © 1972 by Mirra Ginsburg. Reprinted
by permission of Hamish Hamilton Ltd.

Harper & Row, Publishers, Inc., for the art
and adapted text of *And I Mean It, Stanley,* written and illustrated by Crosby Bonsall. Copyright
© 1974 by Crosby Bonsall. By permission of
Harper & Row, Publishers, Inc., and of World's
Work Ltd, England. Also for the text and art of
"Little Bear Goes to the Moon" from *Little Bear*
written by Else Holmelund Minarik, illustrated by
Maurice Sendak. Text Copyright © 1957 by Else
Holmelund Minarik. Pictures Copyright © 1957
by Maurice Sendak. An *I Can Read* Book. By
permission of Harper & Row, Publishers, Inc.,
and of World's Work Ltd, England.

Macmillan Publishing Company for "The
Chick and the Duckling" by Mirra Ginsburg.
Adapted with permission of Macmillan Publishing Company from *The Chick and the Duckling*
by Mirra Ginsburg. Copyright © 1972 by Mirra
Ginsburg. Also for "The Little Turtle" by Vachel
Lindsay. Reprinted with permission of Macmillan Publishing Company from *Collected Poems*
by Vachel Lindsay. Copyright 1920 by Macmillan
Publishing Company, renewed 1948 by Eliza-
beth C. Lindsay.

Illustrators and Photographers: Linda Post,
Kristen Dietrich, Post & Co., 1–7, 38–39,
74–75, 113–115, 157, 174–176; Cathy Bennett,
8–17, 37; Phyllis Graber Jensen, 18–19;
Crosby Bonsall, 20–25; Michael L. Pateman,
26–31, 40–49, 116–118, 130, 138–140,
154–157; B. F. Stahl, 32–35, 37; Brian Sisco,
36, 72, 112; Giulio Maestro, 50–55, 73; Frank
Asch, 56–61, 70–71; Jerry Pinkney, 62–69;
Lucinda E. McQueen, 76–81, 113; Stephen
Ogilvy, 82–89; Maxie Chambliss, 90–93,
141–153; Nancy Edwards-Calder, 94–103, 113;
Roz Schanzer, 104–113; Jacqueline Chwast,
119–129; David McCall Johnston, 131–137;
Dianne Cassidy, 156; Maurice Sendak,
158–173.

Design, Ginn Reading Program:
Creative Director: Peter Bradford
Art Director: Gary Fujiwara
Design Coordinator: Anne Todd
Design: Lorraine Johnson, Linda Post, Kevin
Young, Cathy Bennett, Kristen Dietrich

Contents

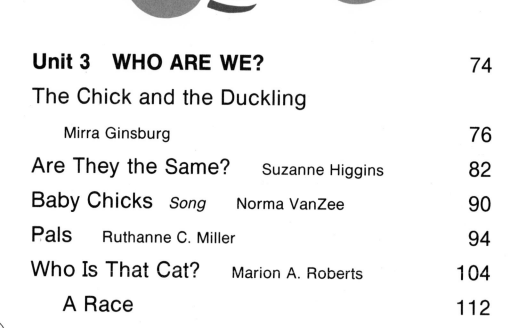

A Little Work, A Little Play

7

A Fish Out of Water

Stephen Elliot

What do you like to do on a
beautiful day? I like to go swimming.
I am good at swimming.
Dad and Mom say I look like
a fish in the water.

Yesterday was not a beautiful day.
Yesterday was not a good day for swimming.
" You are like a fish out of water, "
said Dad. " What are you going to do ? "
" You'll see, " I said.

9

"Dad, you can come in now," I said.
"I made some fish.   This is a cat fish.
I made another fish.   It's a dog fish.
Here is another fish.   This is a pig fish."

"I see," said Dad.   "You made some
fish out of water. I'll make another fish."

"Dad, what fish will you make?"
I asked.

"You'll see," said Dad.

This is the fish my dad made.

Yesterday was a beautiful day for
this fish out of water.

A Day with Grandpa Stephen Elliot

I didn't go swimming, yesterday.
Yesterday was not a good day for swimming.
But now it's a beautiful day.
    " Mom, now may we go swimming ? "
I asked.
    " It's a great day for swimming, "
Mom said. " But we are going for a train ride.
We are going to see your grandpa.
We can all go swimming another day. "

" Listen, do you hear the bell ? "
asked Mom. " It's time for the train to go.
What do you see out there ? "

" I can see a little dog with a big bone, "
I said. " Look, Mom ! There's a
big man on a little bike. "

" Listen, " said Mom. " Do you hear the
bell now ? It's time for the train to stop. "

" Here's Grandpa, " said Mom.

" Did you like your train ride ? " Grandpa asked.

" The ride was great ! " I said.

" Come with me, and we can all talk, " said Grandpa. " You can tell me what you saw on your ride. "

I like to talk and listen to Grandpa.

"I'll make some bread for you,"
Grandpa said. "Talk to me as I make
the bread. Here is some bread mix."

"Grandpa, the bread mix looks like
clay," I said. "I can make it look
like something. Don't look, Grandpa."

15

Mom can hear Grandpa and me.

" I want to see what you are doing, "
she said. " What did you make? "

" You and Mom can look now, " I said.

" What's all of this? " asked Grandpa.
" I see a little dog with a big bone.
There is a great, big man on a little bike. "

" See, Grandpa, " I said.
" This is what we saw on the train! "

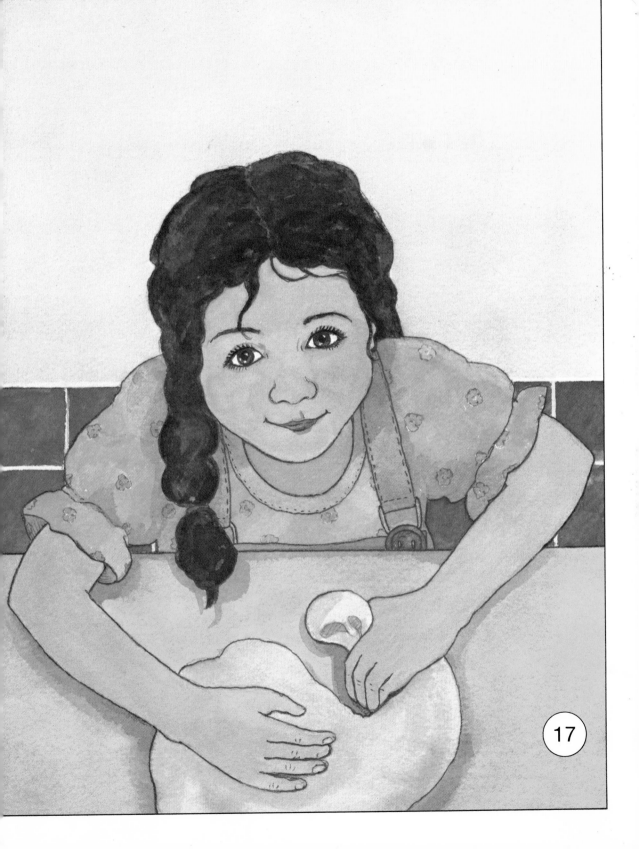

17

Grandpa

Grandpa, will you talk with me?
I like to be with you.
I like the stories that you tell,
The special things we do.

I like the walks we take together,
The special things we see.
And I just like to be with you—
So will you sit and talk with me?

Carolyn Joyce

19

And I Mean It, Stanley

Crosby Bonsall

Listen, Stanley.
I know you are there.
I know you are in back of the fence.

But I don't care, Stanley.
I don't want to play with you.
I don't want to talk to you.

You stay there, Stanley.
Stay in back of the fence.
I don't care.

I don't need you, Stanley.
And I mean it, Stanley.

I am making a great thing, Stanley.
I know you will want to see it.
Well, you can't.
And I mean it, Stanley.

I don't want you to see
what I am making.
Stay in back of the fence.
Don't you look. Do you hear me, Stanley?

   This thing I am making is neat.

It is all made now.

It is the best thing I ever made.

   But don't look, Stanley.

I don't want you to see it.

And I mean it . . .

STANLEY!

Aw, Stanley.

Finders Keepers   Miriam Cohen

" Look what I found ! " Carlos said.
" I found this big, beautiful ball ! "

Jeff said, " Look what Carlos found ! "

Sammy said, " Carlos, that's not your ball. It's my ball. I lost it yesterday. "

" I found this ball, " said Carlos.
" It's my ball now ! "

" Finders Keepers, " said Jeff.

" My dad gave that ball to me, " said Sammy. " I want it back ! "

" Maybe you lost another ball, " Carlos said.

27

Jeff said to Sammy, " Finders Keepers. Losers Weepers. "   Sammy was crying.

" Sammy, is this your ball ? " asked Julia.
" Yes ! " said Sammy.

" Carlos, is this your ball ? " asked Julia.
" Yes ! " said Carlos.

Carlos said, " My grandma gave me
a ball. It looked like this ball.
I lost the ball at my grandma's house.
Maybe my ball rolled here from
my grandma's house! "

Carlos said, " My dog can find
the way home. She can
find the way home from
my grandma's house. "

" Yes, she can, " Julia said.
" But a ball isn't a dog.
Can a ball find the way home ? "

Carlos wished and wished.
He wished he did not know that Sammy
lost that ball! He had to do something he
didn't want to do.

" Here, " he said.

He looked at the big, beautiful ball.
And he gave the big, beautiful ball to Sammy.

Work and Play   Walker Stewart

We know there is work,
and there is play.
Can work be play?
Can play be work?
Let's find out.

This man is making something for his house. He's making a great, big fence.

Find another fence and another house. Have you found the little fence?

She's making this fence for a doghouse.

Is this work? Is this play?

Great! We can all go out.

Some of us will talk. Can you find us?

Some of us will listen. We want to hear

what's going on. We like to play this way.

Who will talk now?

We can listen and hear what she will say.

Is this work? Is this play?

We are making something beautiful.

All of us have found something to do.

We all like what we are doing.

Maybe this is work. Maybe this is play.

What have you found out?

Do you know what is work and what is play?

Maybe the same thing can be work and play. 35

Step on It

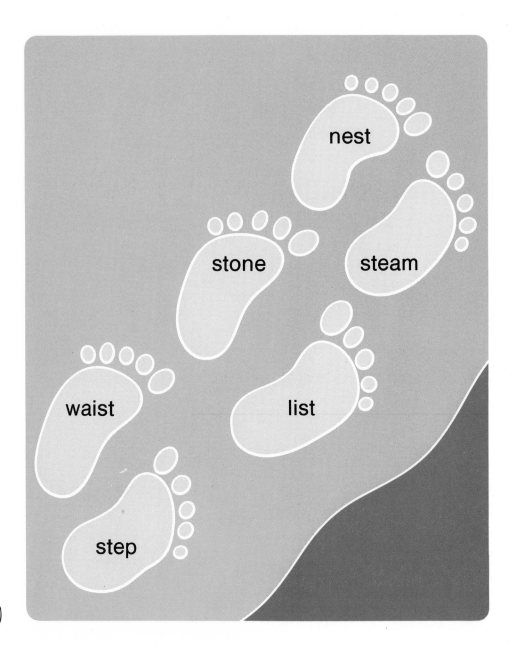

nest

stone steam

waist list

step

Can It Be?

Grandpa can bake bread.

Stanley can talk.

A ball can find the way home.

Work can be play.

Come and Go

Where are we going? Do you know?

Here we are, and there we go!

Come with Us   Suzanne Higgins

"I am Kim," said Kim.
"Can you find Ben and me?
This is a great place to play!"

"First we climb in," said Ben.
"Then we climb out."

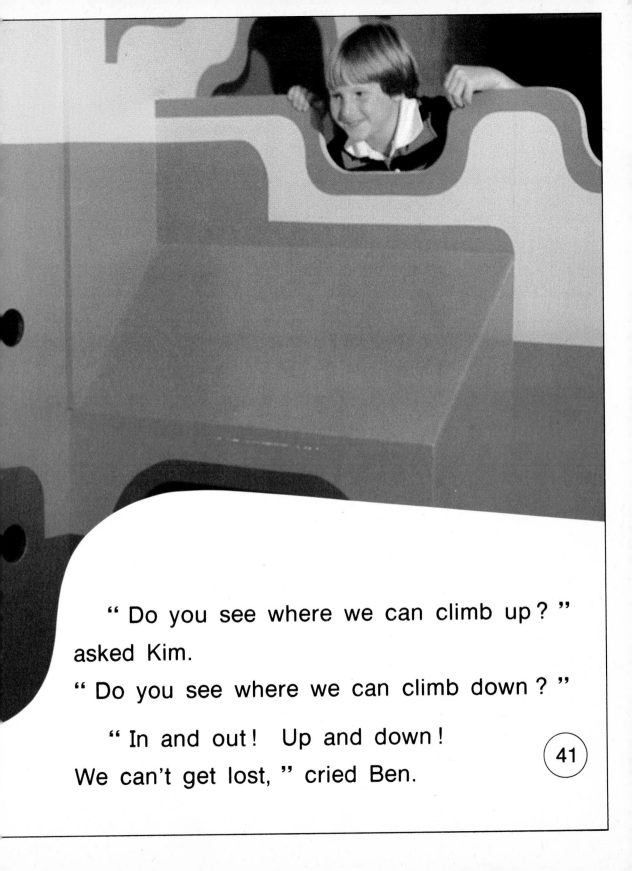

" Do you see where we can climb up? "
asked Kim.

" Do you see where we can climb down ? "

" In and out! Up and down!
We can't get lost, " cried Ben.

" We had to climb down to get here, "
said Kim. " This is a place to work. "

" Is this a good place to swim ? "
asked Ben.

" No, " said Kim. " We can't swim here ! "

" After we work, my mom may take us to
a pond, " said Ben. " We can't swim here.
We can swim at the pond. "

"We will make something here,"
said Kim. "First, Ben has something to do.
He will do it again and again.
After Ben does his work,
I will do my work."

"We'll work to make
something we need," said Ben.

43

" Look at this great house we found ! "
cried Kim.

(44) After we walked into the house, I lost Ben !
I didn't know what happened to Ben !

First, I walked up to look for him.

He was not there.

Then I walked down again.

There was Ben!

" What happened to you ? " I asked.

" I ran down the back way, " Ben said.

" This is a great place to go ! " said Ben.
" First, we saw a place to play. "

" Then we saw a place to work, "
said Kim.

" There was another place to work, "
said Ben. " We made something there. "

" The house was the last place we saw, "
said Kim. " What happened there ? "

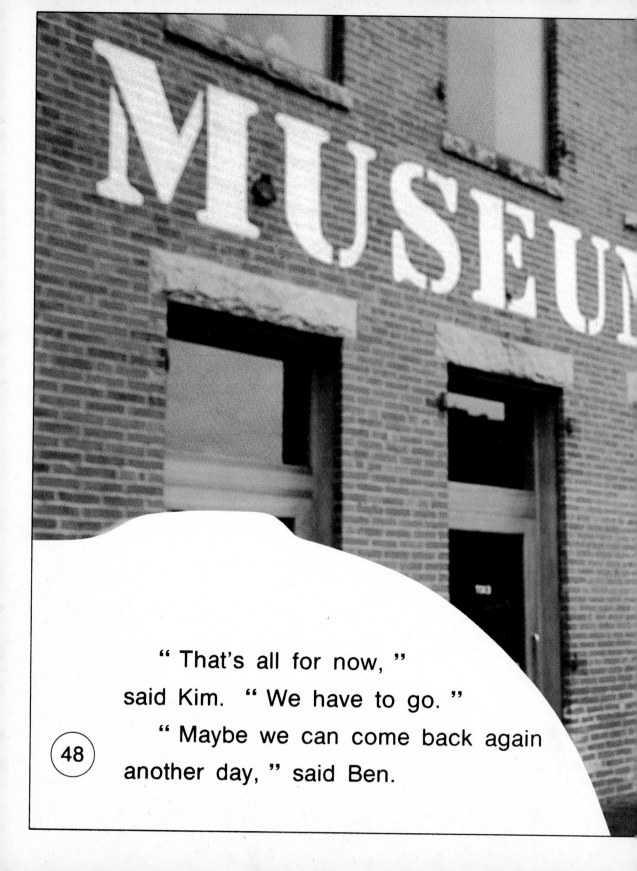

" That's all for now, "
said Kim. " We have to go. "
    " Maybe we can come back again
another day, " said Ben.

48

49

Three Kittens

Mirra Ginsburg

Three kittens—black, gray, and white—
saw a mouse.

They ran after it.

The mouse jumped into a can.

The kittens jumped in after it.

The mouse ran away.

Three white kittens came out of the can.

Three white kittens saw a toad.

They ran after it.

The toad jumped into a pipe.

The kittens went in after it.

The toad jumped away.

Three black kittens came out of the pipe.

Three black kittens saw a fish in the pond. They went in after it.

The fish got away.

Three wet kittens came up from the pond.
The three wet kittens went home.

On the way home, the sun came out.

Again the three kittens became
black, gray, and white.

55

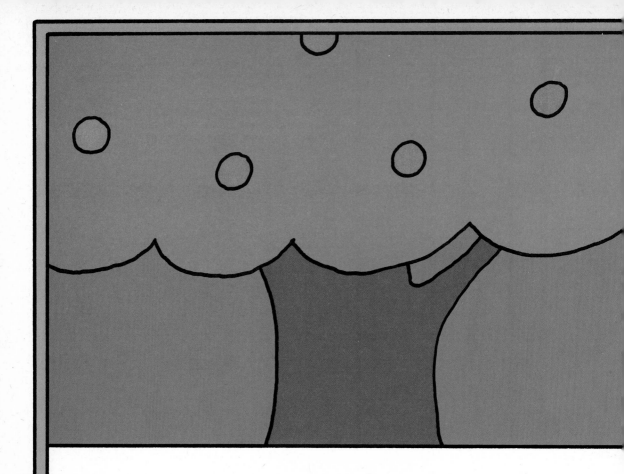

Head In, Head Out   Frank Asch

Turtle walked to the pond for a swim.
On the way home, something happened
to Turtle. Something fell on his head. Plop!

" I am not happy with my head out.
From now on, I will keep my head in, "
he thought.

" That's what a wise turtle would do. "

Turtle walked home with his head in.
He couldn't see where he was going.
He fell into a hole and couldn't climb out.

He thought, " Look what has happened
now. I am not happy with my head in.
And now I can't climb out of here.
What would a wise turtle do now? "

He put his head out and cried, " Help ! "

Bear was the first to hear Turtle.
Bear looked into the hole and saw
Turtle there.

" Why is Turtle in that hole ? "
thought Bear.

59

Bear jumped down into the hole.

Turtle was happy to see Bear!

" Why are you down here? " asked Bear.

" Don't ask me why I am here, "
said Turtle. " Just help me out of
this hole. "

Bear helped Turtle climb out.

As Turtle walked home he thought,
" From now on I will keep my head out—
sometimes. And sometimes, I will keep it in.
Yes, that's what a wise turtle would do. " 61

Fred Is OK   Lynne S. Forman

" May, do you want to play ball? "
asked Hank.

" I would like to play ball, but I
have something to do at home, " said May.
" Maybe we can play ball another day. "

" What's May going to do at home? "
thought Hank.

" Mom, I am home, " cried May.

" I am happy you are here, "
said Mom. " I need your help. "

May saw the three kittens,
the white mouse, and the turtle.

" What would you like me to do first ? "
asked May.

" First, give the three kittens something to
eat, " said Mom. " Then give the white
mouse and the turtle a drink of water. "

Hank asked May to play ball another day.
Again May said, " I can't play ball now.
I have to help my mom. "

May ran all the way home again.

" There is something May can
help me with, " thought Hank.

First, May gave the three kittens
something to eat. Then she went to get some
water for the white mouse and the turtle.

Then May saw Hank.

" What are you doing here ? "
asked May.

" I saw you help your mom yesterday, "
said Hank. " Maybe you can help Fred. "

" Who is Fred ? " asked May.

" Fred is my frog, " said Hank.

" Can you find out why Fred can't swim ? "
asked Hank.

" I'll see what I can do, " said May.

May put Fred in a little water.
Fred did not swim.   He jumped.
He jumped out of the water.
Fred did not look happy.

" Maybe my mom will know why Fred
can't swim, " said May.

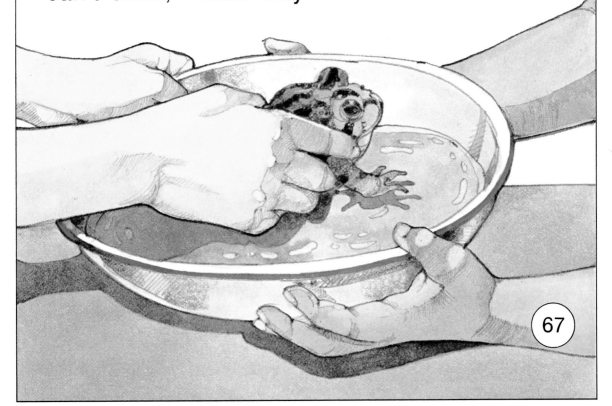

May and Hank went to see May's mom.

" Mom, do you know why this frog can't swim ? " asked May.

" Yes, I do, " said Mom.

" Is Fred OK ? " asked Hank.

" Yes, Fred is OK, " said May's mom. " But Fred is not a frog. Fred is a toad. A toad does not like to swim. "

" I didn't know that Fred was a toad, " said Hank. " I am happy that he is OK. "

" Hank, where's Fred ? " asked May. Fred had jumped away.

" Fred ! Wait for me ! " cried Hank.

The Little Turtle

There was a little turtle.

He lived in a box.

He swam in a puddle.

He climbed on the rocks.

He snapped at a mosquito.

He snapped at a flea.

He snapped at a minnow.

And he snapped at me.

He caught the mosquito.

He caught the flea.

He caught the minnow.

But he didn't catch me.

Vachel Lindsay

71

Look and Find

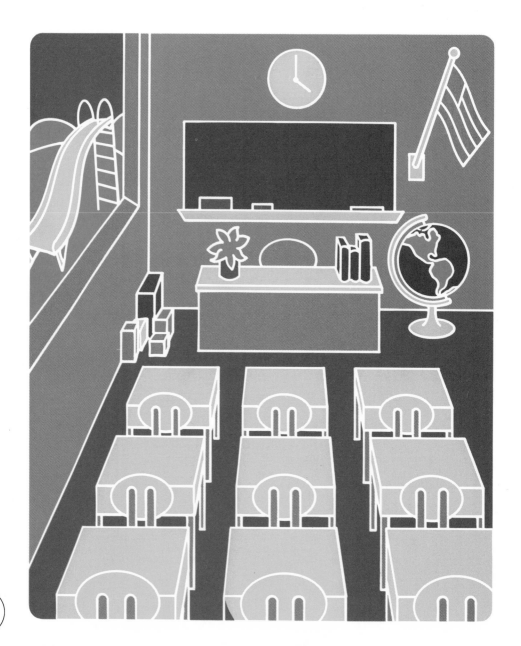

First and Last

What happened first?

What happened last?

73

Who Are We?

I am I, and you are you.

Come find out what we can do!

74

75

The Chick
and the Duckling
Mirra Ginsburg

A Duckling came out of the shell.

" I am out ! " he said.

" Me too, " said the Chick.

" I am going for a walk, " said the Duckling.

" Me too, " said the Chick.

Bailey Gatzert School

77

" I am digging a hole, " said the Duckling.

" Me too, " said the Chick.

" I found a worm, " said the Duckling.

" Me too, " said the Chick.

"I am going for a swim, " said the Duckling.

" Me too, " said the Chick.

" I am swimming, " said the Duckling.

" Me too ! " cried the Chick.

The Duckling helped the Chick out.

80

" I am going for another swim, "
said the Duckling.

" Not me, " said the Chick.

Are They the Same? Suzanne Higgins

You read about a chick and a duckling.
Now you are going to read about
another chick and duckling.

You will find out some ways
a chick and a duckling are the same.

You will find out some ways they are
not the same.

A chick is a bird.

A duckling is a bird, too.

A bird comes from an egg.

Find the big egg.

Do you know who came from that egg?

Did you know it was the duckling?

The chick and the duckling will work to get out of the egg.

After they come out, they will need something to eat. Who will feed the chick? Who will feed the duckling?

Here the chick and the duckling are
digging. Digging is a way to find
something to eat. What are they digging for?

Do you know some ways a chick and
a duckling can get around?
Can they fly?
A chick can't fly, but she can hop.
A duckling can't fly, but he can walk.
A chick and a duckling can run, too.

The duckling can do something the chick can't do. You may know what it is.
The duckling can swim.
Do you know why a duckling can swim?
Look at the duckling's feet. Do the chick's feet look like the duckling's feet?

Some day the duckling will be a duck. The chick will be a hen.

Would the hen like to go swimming with the duck?

Now you know some ways a chick and a duckling are the same.

Do you know some ways they are not the same?

Baby Chicks

Peck, peck, peck !
Oh, see the little chicks
Are cracking all the eggs.
At first you see their tiny beaks
And then their little legs.

2. Peck, peck, peck! The lit-tle chicks are glad To be out in the sun. It won't be long be-fore they're strong, And then just watch them run!

Peck, peck, peck!
The little chicks are glad
To be out in the sun.
It won't be long before they're strong,
And then just watch them run!

Norma VanZee

93

Pals   Ruthanne C. Miller

Kate and Sara are good pals.
They like to play the same games.
They like to read the same books.
They like to walk and talk the same way, too.

" We are good pals, " said Kate.
" The best ! " said Sara.

Kate and Sara like to fly kites.

" Look at the kites fly up, up, up! " said Sara.

" Oh, no! " cried Kate.

" Look at the kites fly down, down, down! "

Kate and Sara like to go digging.
Sometimes, they find something they like.
Sometimes, they find something they don't like.

Sara ran to Kate's house.

" Do you want to go for a walk ? "
asked Sara.   " Maybe we can go digging. "

" No, " said Kate.   " I don't want to go
for a walk now.   My cat had kittens.
Would you like to play with my kittens ? "

" I don't like kittens, " said Sara.

" You don't ? " asked Kate.

" No, I don't ! " said Sara.
" I am going digging ! "

Kate looked at the kittens.

" I like to play with you, " said Kate.

" But I want Sara to be here, too. "

" Oh, this digging is no fun, "
Sara thought. " I want to play with Kate.
Maybe she'll want to go digging now. "

Sara went back to Kate's house.

" Kate, will you come out to play with me now ? " asked Sara.

" Do you want to play with my kittens ? " asked Kate.

Sara saw the kittens.

" Oh ! " said Sara. " The kittens are so little ! " Sara picked up a kitten.

" I have to give away some of my kittens, " said Kate. " Would you like a kitten ? "

" You want to give me a kitten to keep ? " asked Sara.

"Yes," said Kate. "After all, we are good pals."

"The best!" said Sara. "I'll ask my mom and dad about the kitten."

"We can do the same thing sometimes," said Kate.

"But we are best pals all the time!" said Sara.

Who Is That Cat? Marion A. Roberts

Here comes Mrs. Clay.
She's going to work on her bike.

" Happy! Here, Happy! " said Mrs. Clay.
" I have something good for you to eat. "

Mrs. Clay likes to call me Happy.
What does she have for me to eat?
I'll take a walk and see.

Oh, good! Mrs. Clay has some fish
for me to eat. I do like to eat good fish.
And I do like Mrs. Clay. She's kind to me.
She likes to give me something to eat.
Maybe I'll stay with Mrs. Clay.

See, Bird!

I don't have to look for something to eat.

Here comes Jim Bell on his way to school.
Does Jim have something for me to eat?

" Kitten! Here, Kitten! " said Jim.
" I have something good for you to eat. "

Jim likes to call me Kitten.
What does he have for me?

It looks like Jim has an egg for me.
I can't say that I would like to eat an egg.
Bird, would you like to eat this egg?

I may not like this egg, but I like Jim.
He is kind to me.
He likes to give me something to eat.
Maybe I'll stay with Jim.

107

Oh, here comes Pat Gray.
She's going to school, too.
Does she have something for me?
I'll walk to her and see.

" Max! Come here, Max, " said Pat.
" Where are you? I have something good
for you to eat. "

Pat likes to call me Max.
What does she have for me to eat?

What is this? Is it bread?
Oh, I like good bread!
Pat is kind to me.
She likes to give me something to eat.
Maybe I'll stay with Pat.

Now they are all away for the day.
Maybe I'll walk around here all day.

Here comes Mrs. Clay on her bike.
She must be on her way home from work.
" Come here, Happy ! " said Mrs. Clay.

Oh, oh ! Here comes Jim Bell !
" Happy ? That's Kitten ! " said Jim.

Oh, no ! Here comes Pat Gray, too !
" Happy ? Kitten ? That cat is Max ! "
said Pat.

See, Bird.

Happy . . . Kitten . . . Max.

They all like me.

They all give me something to eat.

Maybe I'll stay here for good.

A Race

What's It About?

A Tale for You,
A Tale for Me

Ask me what a tale should be,

I'll tell you, " It's not up to me! "

A fox, a mouse, a bird, a hen ?

It happened now ?   It happened then ?

What Will You Read, Mr. Long?

" Here comes Mr. Long, " said Ms. Gomez.

" What are you going to read to us,
Mr. Long ? " asked Jeff. " Are you going
to read *The Three Bears* ? "

" No, " said Mr. Long. " I am not
going to read *The Three Bears.* "

" Are you going to read
The Little Red Hen ? " asked Jeff.

" No, I am not going to read
The Little Red Hen, " said Mr. Long.

" What are you going to read, Mr. Long ? "
asked Jeff.

" I am going to read you a book about a
rabbit , " said Mr. Long.

" First, I'll tell you about the book. "

There is something in Rabbit's house.
Is it a fox ?   Is it a mouse ?
Do you know what it will be ?
Listen now and you will see.

Rabbit
and the
Long One

A Masai folktale

119

Rabbit came home from work.
She was happy to be home.
But what was this?
Rabbit could not get in her house!
Something was in Rabbit's house!

" Who is there? " cried Rabbit.

" Who is in my house? "

"I am the Long One," something said.
"All are afraid of me because I am great.
This is my house now! Go away!"

This made Rabbit afraid.
She went to get help.

Rabbit found Dog.

" Something is in my house, "
Rabbit said. " Come and help me. "

So Dog went to Rabbit's house.

" Who is in Rabbit's house ? " he asked.

" I am the Long One, " something said.
" All are afraid of me because I am great.
This is my house now ! Go away ! "

Dog was afraid. But he said,
" I know what we can do !
We can make a fire.
That will get rid of the Long One ! "

" That will get rid of my house, too ! "
said Rabbit. " No, no. We can't do that ! "

So Rabbit and Dog went to get help.

Rabbit and Dog found Elephant.

" Something is in my house, "
Rabbit said. " Come and help me. "

So Elephant went to Rabbit's house.

" Who is in Rabbit's house ? " she asked.

" I am the Long One, " something said.
" All are afraid of me because I am great.
This is my house now ! Go away ! "

Elephant was afraid.
But she said, " I am big.
I will walk on your house, Rabbit.
That will get rid of the Long One ! "

" That will get rid of my house, too ! "
said Rabbit. " No, no.
You can't do that ! "

By now, Rabbit did not know what
to do. Dog could not help her.
Elephant could not help her. They were
all afraid. Who could help her?

Just then, Frog came by.

" I can help you, " Frog said.

" You, Frog ? " asked Rabbit.

" How can you help ? You are too little. "

" You will see ! " said Frog.

Frog went up to Rabbit's house.
" Who is in Rabbit's house ? " she asked.
    " I am the Long One, " something said.
" All are afraid of me because I am great.
This is my house now ! Go away ! "
    " I will not go away ! " said Frog.
" I am the Great One. I can do
what I want. I can get in that house.
And I can get you ! Come out !
You will not like what I can do. "

Little by little something came out of
Rabbit's house. What was it?

It was a long, long caterpillar.
He looked around.

"Where is the Great One?"
asked the caterpillar.

"I am just a little thing. I don't want
the Great One to get me. I'll go away."

" A caterpillar ! " said Rabbit.
" We were afraid of a caterpillar !
Frog, how come you were not afraid ? "

" Your house is not big, " said Frog.
" So how could something great and big
be in it ? "

Read Us Another Book

" Mr. Long, " said June, " it was fun to hear the book about Rabbit. Will you read us another book ? "

" Yes, I will, " said Mr. Long. " First, you will see something from the book. "

" There must be a bird, " said June.

" Yes, " said Mr. Long. " Now, you will find out about this bird. "

The Nightingale

adapted from the tale by Hans Christian Andersen

Long ago, there was an emperor. He was a happy man because of his nightingale.

This nightingale was a little bird. She did not look beautiful, but she sang beautiful songs.

Everyone would come to hear the songs. They would listen all day because the songs were happy songs.

One day, someone gave the emperor another nightingale. It was a toy nightingale. The toy bird could not fly, but it could sing. It sang one tune again and again. Everyone could sing the tune with the toy nightingale. Best of all, the toy nightingale was beautiful to look at.

Now everyone thought the toy nightingale was the best.

The real nightingale was not happy.
She went back to her tree.
Everyone just looked at
the toy nightingale.
They did not care about
the real nightingale.
They did not care because they
could listen to the toy
all day long.

One day, the toy nightingale
did not work. The wheels
did not go around.
The emperor was afraid that
the toy nightingale would not
work again. He asked for
someone to help.

A man came and made the
toy run again.

" Take care, " said the man.
" The toy nightingale must not
sing all day long, day after day.
It may stop again for good. "

Now it happened that the
emperor was not well one day.
Everyone came to help.
They gave the emperor
one thing, then another.
Not one thing helped.

All were afraid the emperor
would not get well.
The emperor just wanted
to hear the song of
the nightingale.

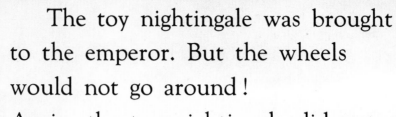

The toy nightingale was brought
to the emperor. But the wheels
would not go around!
Again, the toy nightingale did not work.

Everyone thought the toy nightingale
would help the emperor.
Now they did not know what to do.
They were sad because they could not
help the emperor.

Just then, the real nightingale
came in. She sang one song.
Then she sang another song.
The little bird sang
beautiful songs all day.

Now the emperor was happy again.
The little nightingale came back
day after day. And with her help the
emperor became
well again.

" Did you like the book about
the nightingale ? " asked Mr. Long.

" Oh, yes ! " said June.
" I was happy that the nightingale
came back. Will you read us
another book, Mr. Long ? "

" I would like to read to you,
but I must go now, " said Mr. Long.
" I'll come back another day. "

Mr. Long Is Back!

" Mr. Long is back ! " said Jean.

" Will you read to us again, Mr. Long ? "

" Yes, " said Mr. Long.

" First, I'll tell you another rhyme.

This rhyme will tell you about the book. "

Who can fit in a mitten ?

How about a little kitten ?

Did I hear someone say a pig ?

I hope the pig is not too big.

No Room!

It was a cold, cold day.
A mouse was looking for a warm spot.
Just then, the mouse saw
something by a tree.
It was a mitten, just one mitten.

141

"That looks like a good, warm home," the mouse said.
"I'll just get in it to stay warm."
The mitten was just right for a mouse.

Then a bird came by. She was so cold.
And the mitten looked warm.

" That looks like a good, warm home, "
the bird said.

" I'll just get in it to stay warm. "

" There is no room, " said the mouse.

" I am so cold, " said the bird.

" Well, maybe I can find
a speck of room for you, " said the mouse.

The bird got into the mitten.
The mitten was not just right now.

Then a rabbit came to the mitten. She
was so cold.   And the mitten looked warm.
    " That looks like a good, warm home, "
the rabbit said.
" I'll just get in it to stay warm. "
    " There is no room ! " said the bird.
    " I am so cold, " said the rabbit.
    " OK, we'll find room, " said the bird.
    " That's the last one, " said the mouse.
There was very little room in

the mitten now.

Then a fox came to the mitten. He was
so cold.   And the mitten looked warm.

"That looks like a good, warm home,"
the fox said. "I'll just get in it."

"There is no room!" said the rabbit.

"I am so cold," said the fox.

"OK, we'll find room," said the rabbit.

"That's the last one!" said the mouse.

The fox was too big for the mitten.

But everyone made room.

And the fox went in.

Then a pig came to the mitten.
He was big, and he was cold.
The mitten looked warm.

" That looks like a good, warm home, "
the pig said. " I'll just get in it to
stay warm. "

" There is no room! " said the fox.

" I am so cold, " said the pig.

" OK, we'll find room, " said the fox.

" That's the last one! " said the mouse.

Now there was no room at all in
the mitten. But everyone made room.

And the pig went in.

Then a bear came to the mitten.
He was very, very big. And he was
very, very cold. The mitten looked warm.

"That looks like a good, warm home,"
the bear said.

"I'll just get in it to stay warm."

"No room!" cried the pig and the fox.

"No room!" cried the rabbit and
the bird.

"No room!" cried the mouse.

"Then make room!" said the bear.
Everyone did. And the bear went in. 147

Then a little fly came to the mitten.
She was oh, so cold.
And the mitten looked warm.

" That looks like a good, warm home, "
the fly said.

" I'll just get in it to stay warm. "
Well, there was room for the mouse.
There was room for the bird and the rabbit.
There was a little room for the fox and
the pig. The bear just made it in.

But that was all the mitten could take.

Rip!
Rip, rip!
Rip, rip, rip!
Mitten flew here! Mitten flew there!
Everyone flew out of the mitten!

149

The mouse looked at the bird.
The bird looked at the rabbit.
The rabbit looked at the fox.
The fox looked at the pig.
The pig looked at the bear.
Then everyone looked at the little fly.
    The little fly said, " I have to go now. "
    Then everyone went to find
another home. And there was just
mitten here and mitten there.

151

152

" A fox can't fit in a mitten, " said Jean.

" You are right, " said Mr. Long.

" A real fox can't fit in a real mitten.
Some tales are just for fun. "

" Do you have another book for us ? "
asked Jean.

" I would like to read another book, "
said Mr. Long. " But I must go now.
We have had some fun with tales.
When I come back, we will have
some fun with a rhyme. "

153

Fun with Rhyme

" I am going to read a rhyme you may know, " said Mr. Long. " Then we'll see what fun we can have with this rhyme. "

Hickory, dickory, dock,
The mouse ran up the clock.
The clock struck one,
The mouse ran down,
Hickory, dickory, dock.

" Do you know this rhyme? "
asked Mr. Long.

Hickory, dickory, dook,
The mouse looked in a book.
The mouse said, " Hey!
What does this say?
I don't know a C from an A! "

" You may want to make up
a rhyme, too, " said Mr. Long.
" It's a great way to have
some fun. "

155

Sail Away

speak

spill

spot

spin

speed

What Happened?

Rabbit and the Long One

The Nightingale

No Room!

Little Bear
Goes to the Moon

Else Holmelund Minarik

Pictures by Maurice Sendak

" I have a new space helmet.
I am going to the moon, "
said Little Bear to Mother Bear.
" How ? " asked Mother Bear.

" I'm going to fly to the moon, "
said Little Bear.
" Fly ! " said Mother Bear.
" You can't fly. "

" Birds fly, " said Little Bear.
" Oh, yes, " said Mother Bear.
" Birds fly, but they don't fly to
the moon. And you are not a bird. "
" Maybe some birds fly to the moon,
I don't know.
And maybe I can fly like a bird, "
said Little Bear.

" And maybe, " said Mother Bear,
" you are a little fat bear cub
with no wings and no feathers. "

" Maybe if you jump up
you will come down very fast,
with a big plop. "
" Maybe, " said Little Bear.
" But I'm going now.
Just look for me up in the sky. "
" Be back for lunch, "
said Mother.

Little Bear thought.
I will jump from a good high spot,
far up into the sky,
and fly up, up, up.

I will be going too fast
to look at things,
so I will shut my eyes.

Little Bear climbed to the top of
a little hill.
Then he climbed to the top of
a little tree.
He shut his eyes and jumped.

Down, down he came with a big plop,
and down the hill he tumbled.
Then he sat up and looked around.
" My, my, " he said.
" Here I am on the moon. "

" The moon looks just like the earth.
Well, well, " said Little Bear.
" The trees here look just like our trees.
The birds look just like our birds. "

" And look at this, " he said.
" Here is a house that looks
just like my house.
I'll go in and see what kind
of bears live here. "

" Look at that, " said Little Bear.
" Something to eat is on the table.
It looks like a good lunch for
a little bear. "

Mother Bear came in and said,
" But who is this?
Are you a bear from Earth? "
" Oh, yes, I am, " said Little Bear.
" I climbed a little hill,
and jumped from a little tree.
I flew here, just like the birds. "

" Well, " said Mother Bear.
" My little bear did the same thing.
He put on his space helmet
and flew to Earth.
So I guess you can have his lunch. "

Little Bear put his arms
around Mother Bear.
He said, " Mother Bear, stop fooling.
You are my Mother Bear,
and I am your Little Bear.
We are on Earth, and you know it.
Now may I eat my lunch ? "

" Yes, " said Mother Bear,
" and then you will have your nap.
For you are my little bear,
and I know it. "

New Words in This Book

The following new words are presented in *Birds Fly, Bears Don't,* Level 5, Ginn Reading Program. Words printed in regular type are new Basic words. Those underlined are Enrichment words, and those printed in color are new words that pupils can decode independently.

UNIT 1

8. of
   beautiful
   swimming
   say
9. yesterday
   was
   you'll
10. another
   it's
12. didn't
   grandpa
   great
   your
   all
13. listen
   hear
   time
   there's
   stop
14. talk
   tell
   saw

15. as
16. what's
20. Stanley
   know
   fence
   care
21. stay
22. making
   well
23. neat
   best
   ever
25. aw
26. Finders
     Keepers
   found
   Carlos
   Jeff
   Sammy
   that's
   lost
27. gave
   maybe

28. Losers
     Weepers
   crying
   Julia
   yes
29. looked
   grandma's
   house
   rolled
30. find
   way
   home
   isn't
31. wished
   had
32. be
   let's
33. his
   he's
   she's
   doghouse
35. same

174

UNIT 2

40. Kim
    Ben
    <u>place</u>
    first
    climb
41. down
    <u>lost</u>
    cried
42. swim
    after
    pond
43. again
44. walked
    into
    happened
45. him
46. ran
47. saw
    last
50. three
    kittens
51. black
    gray
    white
    mouse
    they
    jumped
52. away
    came
53. toad
    pipe

went
55. got
    wet
    home
    sun
    became
56. <u>head</u>
    Turtle
    fell
    plop
57. happy
    keep
    thought
    wise
    would
58. <u>couldn't</u>
    hole
59. <u>Bear</u>
    why
60. <u>ask</u>
    just
    helped
61. sometimes
    yes
62. Fred
    OK
    Hank
63. <u>give</u>
    drink
66. frog
68. <u>May's</u>

where's
wait

UNIT 3

76. Chick
    Duckling
    <u>shell</u>
    too
77. <u>walk</u>
78. <u>digging</u>
    <u>worm</u>
82. <u>read</u>
    about
    ways
83. bird
    comes
    an
    egg
84. feed
85. digging
86. around
    fly
    <u>walk</u>
87. <u>duckling's</u>
    feet
    <u>chick's</u>
88. duck
95. pals
    Kate
    games
    books

175

walk
96. kites
97. oh
<u>no</u>
99. <u>Kate's</u>
101. fun
she'll
102. <u>so</u>
picked
kitten
give
103. ask
104. <u>Mrs.</u>
<u>her</u>
likes
105. <u>kind</u>
106. <u>school</u>
108. Pat
Max
110. must

UNIT 4
116. Mr.
Long
<u>Ms.</u>
<u>Gomez</u>

<u>bears</u>
no
red
118. rabbit
<u>Rabbit's</u>
119. One
120. could
her
121. afraid
because
122. so
<u>fire</u>
rid
123. <u>Elephant</u>
124. by
were
125. how
127. <u>caterpillar</u>
130. June
131. <u>nightingale</u>
ago
<u>emperor</u>
sang
<u>songs</u>
everyone
132. someone

gave
<u>toy</u>
sing
tune
133. real
tree
134. stop
135. wanted
<u>song</u>
136. <u>brought</u>
sad
140. rhyme
fit
<u>mitten</u>
hope
141. <u>room</u>
<u>cold</u>
looking
<u>warm</u>
spot
142. <u>right</u>
143. speck
144. <u>very</u>
149. rip
<u>flew</u>
153. tales

BCDEFGHIJ0898765